T0103605

Spiritual Reflections and Some Not So

KATHLEEN CARLSON

WESTBOW°
PRESS
A DIVISION OF THOMAS NELSON
& ZONDERVAN

All scriptures and Biblical references are taken from the
Authorized King James Version of the Holy Bible.

Cover and interior photography by Vernon M. Carlson.

WestBow Press books may be ordered through booksellers or by contacting:

WestBow Press
A Division of Thomas Nelson & Zondervan
1663 Liberty Drive
Bloomington, IN 47403
www.westbowpress.com
1 (866) 928-1240

ISBN: 978-1-4908-6052-7 (sc)
ISBN: 978-1-4908-6053-4 (e)

Library of Congress Control Number: 2014920525

Print information available on the last page.

WestBow Press rev. date: 03/18/2015

Spiritual Reflections and Some Not So

Dedication

To my mother,
Pansy Hill Bunyan,
who first taught me
to love God.

Contents

About the Book

*J*n Kathleen Carlson's new poetry collection, *Spiritual Reflections and Some Not So*, she offers the reader contemplative verse to nourish the soul on many levels. The poet approaches the concept of faith with honesty, humor and a vivid use of language. In, "if who should come tomorrow?" Carlson shares a serious message, rendered with great humor: "... and we/ were going to stop at Phil and Irene's for/ a cocktail later. Sorry, I'm really going to/ be just too busy. Could this Christ fellow/ make it Thursday?"

Carlson reminds us that every moment teaches us something – that life is precious. Each exchange with human, animal or environment is an acknowledgment of this beautiful truth. In the poem, "Friday Afternoon," the speaker lays herself bare, expressing thankfulness for living. Carlson captures the tenderness of how fleeting life is with the lines, "All it needed was a second/ or two more and it would have cleared/ the lanes and made it safely home," and the last line, "I wish the bird had lived."

In her poem, "An Understanding," Carlson gently walks us to our faith, which was there all the time. For those still searching, she woos us with the power of acceptance, which God gives so freely: "God's love is not merit-based -/ It is unconditional." In this faith-based poetry collection, Kathleen Carlson opens up the discussion of what it means to have a true connection to God's love.

—Cristina M. R. Norcross, author of *Land & Sea: Poetry Inspired by Art, The Red Drum, Unsung Love Songs, The Lava Storyteller,* and *Living Nature's Moments: A Conversation Between Poetry and Photography;* Managing Editor of *Blue Heron Review.*

*I*n her project, *Spiritual Reflections and Some Not So,* Kathleen Carlson takes the reader on a faith journey. In the voice of an innocent child, Carlson explores a faith that is poetic, humorous, loving and deeply felt. These deceptively simple poems reflect an abiding faith and an everyday relationship with her Lord whom she talks with as though he were a much loved brother—even a brother whose actions don't always please her.

—Carroll Grossman, author of *Possibility...Yes;* Founding Member, Cherokee Roundtable Writers Group, Louisville, KY

*W*e were stirred by Kathleen's poems. Her writings caused us to reflect in ways uncommon to us in our daily life. The poems are a spectrum from short and powerful to lengthy and profound which can link your heart to hers. We were emotionally moved by the one called "Find the Promise" which makes reference to the desperate and heavy hearted world of the man with the withered hand in the Bible whose condition drastically changed. "May I see your poems" tenderized us. This short and gentle one brought memories of our childhood as we were being delicately cherished by one or both parents including God. There was one that impacted us the most called "Don't you think" which magnified even more for us our Lord Jesus's obedience to a higher commission. And we could go on, but instead we invite you to discover and explore for yourself Kathleen's insights that may cause you to think and imagine in your own peculiar way.

—Jose & Carolina Diaz
Laborers of His Harvest Bible Fellowship
El Paso, Texas

Introduction and Acknowledgements

Many people have confessed Jesus Christ as their Lord and believed God raised him from the dead (Rom. 10:9,10). These people received God's gift of holy spirit just as the Apostles received on the day of Pentecost. Having His spirit living in believers enables God to connect and communicate with believers on a personal level not available during Old Testament times.

These poems are the expression of my experiences and my relationship with God as my spiritual Father and Friend.

Now you may be thinking, I sure could write some better poems if I had holy spirit in me, if God was my Father. Go for it! ...Eye hath not seen, nor ear heard, neither have entered into the heart of man, the things that God hath prepared for them that love him (I Cor. 2:9). Make Jesus Christ lord of your life and believe God raised him from the dead. See where this confession can take you!

Thanks to the many Christian Fellowship coordinators who have shared their love of God and knowledge of the rightly divided Word with me over the years I lived in Chicago, Shirley, Palo Alto, Terra Linda, Fort Wayne, Milwaukee, Oconomowoc, and Mission.

Thanks to Sue Hildebrand, President, Accurate Business Communications, Oconomowoc, WI who courageously undertook the word processing of almost 400 of my poems, from which I selected the poems in this book.

Thanks to my husband Vernon, engineer, photographer, painter and musician, who used his heart to help me choose the art for my verses.

Now thanks *be* unto God, which always causes us to triumph in Christ (I Cor. 2:14a).

Purpose

...that ye may know
what is the hope of his calling...

Eph. 1:18b

if who should come tomorrow?

if who should come tomorrow?
oh...well, I really don't think I could go.
I mean, I have so many things to do.
For instance, after I get the children
off to school, I have my Trimnastics class
and my hair appointment at one...
oh, and I have to squeeze in a little shopping,
too. George and I are going out to dinner....
I hope that snippy little sitter is on time
tonight...I mean you just can't be late
at the Shubert...Pagliaci, you know...and we
were going to stop at Phil and Irene's for
a cocktail later. Sorry, I'm really going to
be just too busy. Could this Christ fellow
make it Thursday?

Man, I just couldn't believe it

Man, I just couldn't believe it...the sky just...
I mean, how was I supposed to know it was true?
After all, people have been talking about it for
centuries...Well, no, I guess I really wasn't surprised
when the angels flashed down the streets
and we were left.

vacant and dark

vacant and dark
a pair of shoes on Howard St. look east
a sweater stretches across a bush
a plaid shirt slapflaps against a light pole
where did they go – the people,
the inhabitants of these clothes?
did they join their Lord
in the middle of the air?
Suddenly
He came
and they were gone.
Could I have missed
the joyous shout
the trump of God
the voice of the Archangel?

Lament of One Born Again

God,
I have no poems
left in me now
and I'm bitter
about that, bitter.
I had enjoyed writing them ---
the gut pleasure they gave,
the thrill, the relief
of getting the emotions out.
Oh, how I miss style
and form
and conciseness of
language.
And I'm sick,
so sick,
of being happy all the time.
Give me some pain, God,
pain,
so I can write
a poem
one
more
time.

He said to me

He said to me
a poem,
perhaps six lines,
about a river,
the most beautiful poem
I've ever heard.
It sang.
It glowed, it moved
    like honey,
    a diamond
    and sunshine ---
the poem
God gave him

Photograph by Vernon Carlson

Four strangers burst into my life

Four strangers burst into my life,
    one wore blue, one wore night.
The one in blue helped me
    off the ground
    where the one in night
    had struck me down.
One in white stitched
    my torn face shut
    where the one in night
    had bruised and cut.
Another in white
    replaced the teeth
    that the one in night
    scattered in the street.
Four strangers burst into my life ---
God, bless the three
    with length of days,
    with health,
    with wealth,
    with honor bright,
and curse that bastard
    who wore night.

How can music be so beautiful

How can music be so beautiful
when there is such pain in my heart?
What Master Torturer
    taught birds to sing
    or put into the soul of man
    the melody that makes
    sax or string cry out
    in agon/ecstacy?
God, why shove it in my ear?
Music is a hope deferred,
    desire unfulfilled
    and left to warble
    on a branch.

most of the time

most of the time
you give me crumbs,
cookie crumbs,
but crumbs nonetheless.
once in a while,
a razor slices
out of you,
a tongue of flame
leaps out ---
sssssssttttttt ---
and electrifies
my heart,
a flash of light,
then gone.
and now
you offer me
poems?
GIVE ME THOSE POEMS!
why are you
doing this to me?
(My God, how this man
    tortures me.)
don't you realize
I know?   I know
what a poem
is.

I have

I have
an advocate · an advocate
with the Father, · before the Court,
Jesus Christ, · Craig Miller,
the Righteous · the attorney
a man
standing
with a two-edged
sword
can only
cut.
His words
razor through
my heart,
dividing
filleting
the thoughts
and intents
of it.
Somehow
I feel safe
with him,
and protected.
But
I fear him
and his words.
The sword
hurts
so.

in a moment

in a moment
in a word
he touched me
with amazing tenderness,
excruciating
pleasure/pain tenderness.
the words came out
and seared my heart.
I almost fainted.
Only a poem
could express
the effect.
And only God
had ever done it
to me
before.

I stretch out my arms

I stretch out my arms
to hold beings I cannot see,
to love a Father and a Son
who are spirits, damit, spirits.
God, this is your only failure.
You made me a woman,
a human woman.
I want to hug you.
Why didn't you give yourself
a form that I could snuggle up to?
Why did Jesus Christ take
himself in that lovely resurrected body
up into the heavenlies and away?
Yes, yes, I know: spirits have
no form or comeliness.
Yes, yes, I know: He had to go
to send the promised seed
to believers on earth.
That is no comfort, God.
I want to hold you.

Photograph by Vernon Carlson

don't you think

don't you think
maybe Jesus Christ
had other ambitions.
maybe he wanted
to be a doctor
or a farmer
or a camel trader
or an astronaut.
is there a man alive
who just wants to be
a piece of lamb
on a stick?

I was glad

I was glad
when they said
unto me
'Let us go into the house
of the Lord.'
Yea.
There's no better place
to hide out
than
in the house of the Lord.
It's quiet in there.
And nobody can get you.
It's not that they can't
find you.
They just can't
get you.
There's always
plenty of food and
good books and
this kinda weird
Hebrew furniture.

I asked God once
why he didn't just
have a garage sale.
This is after all
a new administration
and the Chosen Ones
aren't going to use
this stuff
on the Third Heaven and
Earth.
You know what
the Old Geezer said?
It had sentimental value.
And besides, He was saving
it to make a movie
with Indiana Jones.

as the sand

as the sand
which is by the sea shore
innumerable,
so sprang we all out of Adam's loins,
every genus and combination of man,
compacted into one seed,
one blood, one race.
as the sand
which is by the sea shore
innumerable,
so crept we all out of Eve's womb,
every brother and sister of man,
crammed into one egg,
one water, one sack.
I look into the face
of the bigot
prancing
before me and understand
what God hath wrought,
but I don't like it.
No, baby, I don't like it
at all.

I have slept alone

I have slept alone
in an abandoned corral
and awakened
to the clear morning of Colorado
and known God was there.
I have walked along
the edge of the second story
level of highway bridges
with death speeding
around me
and known God was there.
I have worked
in the midst of murderers
and rapists and robbers
and rejoiced knowing
God was there.
And so I know this problem,
this crisis is a small item
to my God.
Shall He who saves
out of the burning fiery furnace
and out of the lion's mouth
ever leave His child alone?

I feel

I feel
that I'm saying
goodbye
to you,
to my yesterways
of living.
Something
doesn't fit right
any more.
I have to move on.
(It is so hard to let go.)
I hate it
when people have
a vision of me
greater than
my own.
(Why do they feel
compelled to share
it with me?)
Their eyes ask
'What are you doing here?'
or 'what are you still
doing here?'
(like maybe I'm
not human.)
What do they think
they see -
the next Mahatma Gandhi,
the next Isaiah
crying in the wilderness?

what

what
have you done
mankind
to deserve
even a single
star

Photograph by Vernon Carlson

Those men

Those men are dangerous.
They have guns and knives
for hearts and eyes
And their seed is wrong.

God

God
be with me
to bless
and heal
in the name
of Jesus Christ.

Find the Promise

Find the promise.
Believe it.
Act on it.
Receive it.
He made it seem so simple then.
There I was in the synagogue
doing the usual Sabbath things...
I didn't know they were going to
kill him for this.
Bunch of bastards, watching him
so they could accuse him.
Would to God I'd known.
I mean, I've lived with this condition
all my life. I could have lived with it
a while longer.
But when he said 'Stand forth',
it was like he called straight
to my heart and all the pain
of a cripple's life
rushed out of me to him
and he took it.
I remembered the pride dying
in my father's eyes every time
he took me out with him as a child.

I could see the anguish in my wife's eyes
as I struggled to make a living,
scorned and ridiculed by these same men.
He looked on his accusers with anger,
being grieved for the hardness of their hearts
and told me
'Stretch forth thine hand.'
Can you believe that?
Stretch forth my hand...
something I had not been able to do
since the day I was born,
something I had longed to do,
something I had tried to do...
stretch forth my hand...
such a little thing,
such a monstrous thing,
such a loving thing
that I stretched it out and
my hand was restored whole as the other.
My God. My God. My God. My God.
For this, they put him out of the synagogue?
For this, they killed him for this?
Lord, I gladly would have remained
a man with a withered hand.

Mark 3:1-5

I followed the devil

I followed the devil
to a deep dark wood
to sit beneath an oak
with a pistol in my lap
He showed me
the disappointment
I'd been to people
all my failures
all the pain I'd brought
all the evil of my deeds
and as I sank
into the blackness
of his eternal night
I heard my mother's voice
(a voice I had not heard
for over thirty years):
'No, Kay, you are a sweet
and gentle flower'
and I took the barrel
from my mouth

Friday Afternoon

A sparrow flew low across three lanes
of traffic and collided
with the windshield of a jeep
and was killed, broken in feathered
pieces. All it needed was a second
or two more and it would have cleared
the lanes and made it safely home.

A man on a bicycle rode against
the traffic which had the green light.
He was nearly hit by a jeep.
The cyclist took offense at
the drivers' horns and screeching brakes.

I saw these. I was in the car behind.
I tried to learn a lesson from this,
            something for my life:
Fly high.   Obey the rules.   Beware of jeeps.

I wish the bird had lived.

After my university class

After my university class,
after three hours
of Plato and Conrad and Bell,
after thirty-two different
student perspectives,
after driving 58 miles
back to Waukesha,
after parking my car
in the building lot
and putting my key
in the door,
there may be a moth
under the porch lamp
speaking to me
of death and life
in the twilight
and I must listen.
This too is education.

May I see your poems

May I see your poems
the Master asked.
My life is a murmur
in the wind
the student said.
But it is precious
to your Maker
the Master replied.

Photograph by Vernon Carlson

I

I
await
the Return
of Christ.
All else
I do
is mere
entertainment.

An Understanding

God's love is not seasonal –
  It is eternal.
God's love is not merit-based -
  It is unconditional.
God's love is not boundable –
  It is limitless.
God's love is not elitist-
  It is freely given to all.

The love of God is without precedent.
The love of God is precedent setting.

Harnessing the Power of Fish Lips

I was talking with God
the other day
about the state of the world,
how people ought to pray...
Said God, "The project
I'm working on today
is harnessing the power of fish lips."

      Huh? What?
      Harnessing the power of fish lips?!?
      Are you forcing fish to act
      in a freaky way
      that will get You in trouble
      with the SPCA?

He saithed beneath his Holy Breath,
"Somebody, please, give me a break!
Will I never live down that talking snake?
Here's a renewable
source of energy
untapped by mankind
for all eternity.

Every time a fish
pulls water between its lips,
'lectricity is released
that could move a thousand ships
that could fly jet planes
through the deep blue sky
'lectricity as easy as apple pie."
    So God, where is the harness,
    and where the tiny bit,
    and God, where are the wires
    for the conduit?
"O, ye of small ideas,"
the Big Guy said,
"henceforth will fish be born
with transmitters in their heads.
It's up to you humans
to make technology
to get the fishy signal
from the fish lips to TV.
Here's to my inspiration
for this Mysterious Way:
Fish Lipps Bar & Grill,
Cornucopia, Wisconsin, USA."

Hundreds Moved with Us

Hundreds moved with us
reading placards of ancient history
gazing at sacred objects
reaching for but not touching
artifacts known to have issued
from the hand of the Creator.
No one spoke.
No one talked.
Few breathed.
A supercharged silence
hung in the air
as people got as close
to God as they physically could:

The Dead Sea Scrolls and the Bible Exhibit,
Milwaukee Art Museum,
July 2011

I Never Read

I never read
a record
of God
ever
kissing people.
David kissed people.
Solomon kissed people
but not God.
I guess He didn't
want to fry them
to a crisp.

It Doesn't Matter

It doesn't matter
when I die.
I know that I know
that I know that I know
I will be with
Jesus Christ at his Return.
It's a promise in God's Word.
However I do care
how I die –
Death by ice cream
is better than
death by chocolate.
Fire is better
than ice.

Photograph by Vernon Carlson

Thanksgiving Poem

We thank You, God,
for all Your care,
eternal life,
Your Word to share,
for love, and joy,
and spiritual peace,
and a future where all pain shall cease,
we thank You.

The Problem

The problem
with God's Word is—
the more you read it
the more you study it
the bigger it gets.

The Scream

the sound of it
shook the garden
the beasts turned their
heads in its direction
birds jumped into the sky
at it
Adam had been naked
and knew it not
Adam had been perfect
and cherished it not
No longer could he stand
before God without any sense
of sin, guilt or condemnation
so he cried out
from the depths of his being ---
the scream heard still.

There Will Be No Bugs in Heaven (Song)

Lyrics and Melody by Kathleen Carlson
Arrangement by Vernon Carlson

Verse One

There will be no bugs in heaven when I die,
Nothing creepy crawly crawling up my thigh,
Nothing stinging, biting, crunching,
sucking, spiting, gnawing, munching,
There will be no bugs in heaven when I die.

Verse Two

There will be no bugs in heaven when I die,
No more chiggers, spiders, 'skeeters in my sky,
Nothing buzzing, whirring, flapping,
diving, flying, clawing, zapping,
There will be no bugs in heaven when I die.

Verse Three

There will be no bugs in heaven when I die,
Nothing there to chew my flesh or drain me dry,
Nothing there to make me itchy,
burn my skin, or drive me bitchy,
There will be no bugs in heaven when I die.

Chorus

Glory, glory, alleluia, Happy Trails to Me, Good Bye!
There will be no bugs in heaven when I die.

About the Author

Kathleen Carlson has been a Born Again Christian and student of the Word of God since 1975. She started writing poetry at age seven. **Spiritual Reflections** *and* **Some Not So** expresses her experiences and relationship with God as a Father and Friend.

Kathleen was born on the island of Aruba, Netherlands Antilles, on June 23, 1946. She was the second child of Arthur and Wilhelmina (Hill) Bunyan, originally of Georgetown, Guyana. The Bunyan family immigrated to Wisconsin in 1953. She became a U.S. citizen in 1974.

She has a BA in English, the University of Wisconsin-Milwaukee, an MS-Journalism, Northwestern University, and an MA in English, the University of Wisconsin-Milwaukee.

She lives with her husband Vernon in Mission, Texas, in the Rio Grande Valley.

Printed in the United States
By Bookmasters